THE GARDENS OF WESTMINSTER ABBEY

JAN PANCHERI

Head Gardener

SCALA

CONTENTS

FOREWORD

GARDENS are not the first thing to spring to mind at the mention of Westminster Abbey. Gothic splendour, the tombs of kings and queens and of the great of our country, but not gardens. I always remember the first time that I discovered Little Cloister, for there was no real lead up to this hidden jewel. Suddenly a cavernous corner is turned and there it is, a green and flowery oasis with water trickling at its heart. This encounter is, I think, what sets the Abbey's various gardens apart. They are all enclosed experiences approached through archways and passages, often at awkward and unexpected angles and in unexpected places, so that almost without exception they retain an element of surprise.

Collectively they make up the oldest horticultural space still under cultivation in central London. Gardens by their very nature are ever-changing works of art, responding both to the prevailing aesthetics and the practical demands of successive ages. Today what we see is the Abbey's response to twenty-first-century mass tourism, aiming to provide it with spaces both for commemoration and celebration and, equally, for rest and contemplation.

Sir Roy Strong, CH, High Bailiff & Searcher of the Sanctuary

INTRODUCTION

WHEN THORNEY ISLAND ON THE NORTH bank of the Thames was chosen, in the tenth century, as the site of a Benedictine monastery, it was not only for its proximity to water for fish and transport, but also for its fertile land. The Rule of St Benedict required that the monks should do physical work, and gardening was an ideal activity, allowing for contemplation while providing healthy outdoor exercise. There was a useful end-product too — beautiful flowers and edible crops. The gardens still exist here, over 1000 years later, kept by gardeners instead of monks, and enjoyed by many locals as well as visitors from all over the world.

Until the dissolution of the monasteries under Henry VIII, the Abbey owned land stretching north to Covent Garden and west to what is now St James's Park. This was used for growing crops such as rye, barley and maslin; and grass to use as animal feed and bedding. Closer to the Abbey, the names 'Abbey Orchard Street' and the former 'Vine Street' reflect the uses of these more local areas. In the medieval period, land outside the City of London was largely agricultural, as the name St Martin-in-the-Fields suggests, and the cultivated areas that

still exist within the Abbey cloisters can be seen as a tiny remnant of this.

Following the dissolution, these gardens no longer retained their individual roles, but they were still used and enjoyed by the resident clergy and the pupils of Westminster School. They may perhaps have inspired some of the illustrious alumni of the school, such as scientist Robert Hooke, dramatist Ben Jonson, composer Henry Purcell and children's author A. A. Milne. During World War II, both gardens and school suffered significant damage, but not destruction.

In this guide, I have concentrated on describing the gardens that the visitor will see as they walk towards and through the cloisters. Most can be viewed whenever the Abbey is open, but others, such as the College Garden, only on specific days. The Abbey gardens are open all year round, which enhances their appeal to the garden visitor. They are intimate gardens, quite unlike a park or other central London outdoor spaces; here each individual garden has its own character.

For us working as gardeners here, history is always at our side. Each morning, as I come to work through the cloisters, I imagine the monks' sandalled feet stepping along the stones. Being in the gardens

Cherry blossom in College Garden (above); Viper's bugloss with the Chapter House roof behind (left)

day after day gives an insider's view of this unique space. In these pages I wanted to capture not only the changing seasons, but also the work we do here, the plants we grow and the wildlife that shares these gardens with us. In writing this book, I aimed to share the story of the gardens of Westminster Abbey with those who may be able to enjoy them only for an hour or two.

Artist's reconstruction of the late-medieval monastery precinct (above); College Garden with Wren's seventeenth-century dormitory wing for Westminster School (below)

GARDEN TIMELINE

960

Community of Benedictine monks established here; they find the Thames 'abounds with fish' and the soil is 'like the fertile plains of Asia'

1222

Abbey's lands include Covent Garden; monks use the church of St Martin-in-the-Fields while they are working the land there

1338

Phillipa of Hainault, wife of Edward III, receives cuttings of a rosemary plant for her garden, now the site of the Jewel Tower

1376

High stone wall, originally thatched, built around Abbey (now College) Garden

1086

Domesday Book; Abbey's lands include 100 acres of forest for keeping pigs

1253

Henry III swears in St Catherine's Chapel to observe the privileges granted in Magna Carta

1371

St Catherine's Chapel built as infirmary chapel for monks

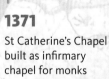

1399

Geoffrey Chaucer living in a house in the garden of the Lady Chapel, replaced by Henry VII's Chapel in 1503

1476

William Caxton sets up first printing press near the Chapter House; he was a parishioner and auditor of St Margaret's church

1560

Queen Elizabeth I re-founds Westminster Abbey and 'Abbey Garden' becomes 'College Garden'

1849

Plane trees planted in College Garden

1929

Greenhouse built in College Garden by Mackenzie and Moncur, 'Hothouse Builders'

2002

Rose Garden created to commemorate the Queen's Golden Jubilee; College Garden fountain installed.

1540

Dissolution of monastery, monks expelled

1560

Abbot Feckenham refuses to leave after the dissolution until he has finished planting elm trees, one for each of his monks, in Abbey Garden

1706

Robert and Anne Southey design and plant Little Cloister Garden

1729

Westminster School dormitory is built in College Garden, designed by Sir Christopher Wren and completed by Lord Burlington

1952

Pupils of Westminster Abbey Choir School perform Shakespeare plays in the ruins of bombed Little Cloister; wartime vegetables grown in garden

2010

HM The Queen opens the Herb Garden to commemorate the refounding of the Abbey as Collegiate Church of St Peter, Westminster

DEAN'S YARD

DEAN'S YARD IS NOW A TRANQUIL area of grass, traditionally used by the Abbey Choir or Westminster School for fetes, or for the odd game of five-a-side football. Attractive buildings housing offices and homes are ranged around it, with spaces for residents' parking. Four large plane trees dominate the area, which also features a red-flowered horse chestnut, a tulip tree, silver birches, a judas tree, rowans and – reflecting its medieval past – a fruit-bearing medlar.

In monastic times, grass occupied about half the space it does today and the rest was cobbled. It was known as 'The Elms', with nine planted here, at a time when elms were the most commonly planted trees in London, much as plane trees are now. This was the Abbot's domain; his home was adjacent and he used this area as his garden, entertaining his guests with pleasant strolls among the shady trees. He is known to have grown damson and pear trees, possibly in his walled garden, where 21 Dean's Yard now stands.

After the Reformation, this became a very different place. Like the Sanctuary, just outside the entrance to Dean's Yard, which by the eighteenth century had shops, stables, cottages and even a tavern or two, so Dean's Yard itself housed a number of retail establishments including a coffee shop and milliner's.

It must have been a bustling place, with horses and carriages rattling over the cobbles. Railings placed around the grass area were removed in 1967, to create a more welcoming impression.

The Victorian Gothic entrance and the houses around it were built in 1853 by George Gilbert Scott, the Abbey's Surveyor of the Fabric. He also introduced the London plane trees, which are now such an important feature of the area and are subject to conservation status. Church House, the Church of England's administrative centre, was rebuilt here in the 1930s, on the site of the monastic bakehouse, the stone foundations of which can still be seen.

Clockwise from left: Dean's Yard in 1793; today; looking towards the gate in 1819; Judas tree in flower; Dean's Yard in 1845

DEANERY COURTYARD

THIS AREA WAS THE COURTYARD to the Abbot's house in monastic times; he had his own private quarters, separate from the monks living in the monastery. In the cobbled space is a fine specimen of a strawberry tree, *Arbutus x andranchnoides*, which has attractive red bark and glossy evergreen leaves, with white bell-shaped flowers in winter. It is a hybrid of our native strawberry tree and the Grecian red-barked one. The 'strawberries' appear more regularly on the English variety but, as its botanical name *Arbutus unedo* suggests, they are not that good to eat.

Six terracotta planters on the flight of steps leading to the Jerusalem Chamber allow us to add colour to the area with seasonal displays. Heathers, cyclamens, clarkia, petunias, pelargoniums, and even some curly kale, have had their moment in these pots. Capacious plant saucers beneath catch the rain and make watering a less regular task. The raised bed is filled with tulips and wallflowers in the spring, and dahlias, coreopsis and helianthus in autumn.

The buildings here, once the Abbot's lodging, now serve as the Deanery. On the left is the medieval College Hall, where the Abbot used to entertain his

Clockwise from far left: view from the entrance; part of the Deanery in the 1880s; colourful planters enliven the steps; the evergreen strawberry tree

guests and which remains part of the Deanery but is now also used during term as one of the dining rooms of Westminster School. The Jerusalem Chamber, with leaded windows and a blackened wooden door, has a ceiling unchanged from the fourteenth century. Under the arch leading to the courtyard is a stone bench, where workmen used to sit and wait for their wages. In the ceiling above are removable circles of stone called 'murder holes', which could be opened up for surprise attacks on undesirables, though there is no record of their ever having been used!

THIS PLAIN SQUARE OF TURF HAS remained relatively unchanged since the Abbey was built. It served the monks who lived and worked here as a green area, where they could walk and quietly contemplate in the fresh air. It was a uniquely sheltered place, being shielded both from the worst of the weather and from the disturbances of the outside world.

The cloister on each side of the garth, a medieval term for garden, was devoted to a particular monastic occupation. The range nearest the Abbey contained partitioned cubicles for reading and study. The south cloister, being near the refectory, was used for washing in preparation for eating. The two or three-storeyed west cloister, which adjoined the entrance area at the West Door, held accommodation for the Abbot's guests. The east cloister contained the monks' dormitory on the upper level, now the Library, while below is the entrance to the thirteenth-century Chapter House.

No-one steps inside the cloister garth now, except to mow the grass or for essential maintenance work. It is peaceful, with only the stone gargoyles to look down on it. The stone tracery of the cloister arcade around it is decorated with patterns of cinquefoil, quatrefoil and trefoil flower or leaf shapes that remind us of wildflowers, such as prunella, silverweed and birds-foot trefoil, which try to re-establish themselves here. For this is now one of the greenest squares in London with a state-of-the-art irrigation system.

At the time of writing, a fountain commemorating the work of the landscape gardener Capability Brown is being planned as a centrepiece for this area.

The Great Cloister has always been a green area; the stone tracery of the arcades echoes the leaf-shape of the little cinquefoil

LITTLE CLOISTER GARDEN

THIS GARDEN IS APPROACHED from the Dark Cloister and glows like a jewel from behind its ornamental gilded gate. The morning sun lights up the green (or, in autumn, the fruit-salad tinged) foliage of the virginia creeper, *Parthenocissus quinquefolia*, which makes a welcoming sight as I am coming into work. The pleasant sound of a trickling fountain and the perfume of iris, lilies or jasmine reaches me before I even get to this sheltered spot.

In monastic times, this area was part of the infirmary and had rooms around it for convalescing and aged monks; now the doorways lead to residents' homes or Abbey offices. We don't have a record of its original layout, but it may very well have been an enclosed garden as now, with a water cistern rather than a fountain.

The first written evidence, by Robert Southey, the Abbey's Head Gardener, records its planting in 1706; in neat handwriting, he notes roses, jasmine, holly, box and *Phillyrea*. Shortly after planting, it seems that a length of box hedging was stolen and had to be replaced, and railings and a gate were later added as protection. The white marble fountain dates from 1836. Just over a hundred years later, in 1941, an incendiary bomb destroyed the walls of the Little Cloister but the fountain survived. The square pond around it now contains goldfish.

The Little Cloister Garden was one of my first challenges as Head Gardener. Two of the walls were

Clockwise from left: Star of Bethlehem; ivy-covered walls in the 1950s; garden seen through virginia creeper; in winter; and in summer

From left: tobacco plant; alliums;
foxgloves; angelica and allium framing
the entrance to St Catherine's Chapel
Garden; fountain with clipped box

completely covered in ivy. While rather splendid in a gothic sort of way, the aerial roots had taken hold of the stonework and ground roots filled the narrow borders, leaving room for little else. In the ivy-clad darkness, a snail colony had taken up residence in large numbers – so much so that their nightly feasts stripped any new plants to stumps. It was a problem only remedied by putting up ladders and attacking the ivy with loppers; we removed two skip-loads of greenery and the walls could then be repaired.

Starting afresh, we dug 50 bags of manure into the poor soil; the resulting pungent aroma was amplified in the enclosed space, as you can imagine. Then we set to work planting the garden to achieve visual symmetry, despite the borders facing in four different directions – one has sun all day, another shade. We removed two broadleaf *Griselinia littoralis* shrubs, which had become too large for their surroundings, and decided to keep plants to a size that would not interrupt the pattern of the stone arcading. We now have either a green and white scheme or a pastel one punctuated with yew cones, and with scented flowers in season. The central lawn has also been levelled and relaid, so that formality and order have been restored.

Winter/spring for hellebores; April and May for iris; summer for lavender and taller flowers; autumn for the Virginia creeper

Magnolia stellata masks the Victoria Tower; the borders (right); column bases and mown lawns (far right)

ST CATHERINE'S CHAPEL GARDEN

THIS AREA, OF ALL THE ABBEY'S green spaces, has probably seen the greatest change. The garden was created in the 1960s, when the area was rebuilt after bomb damage; now, with its neatly-striped lawn instead of tiles, and sky instead of a vaulted roof, it takes a leap of imagination to believe there was ever a building here. The remains of columns and archways, steps and altars, a stone wall scratched with maker's marks and evidence of windows, give us an idea of what the chapel looked like. We also know that it was used by the monks as part of the infirmary at one time — I like to think its present manifestation is a more pleasant place to be!

From a garden design point of view, what we have been left with is a rectangular walled garden, extremely sheltered, with a raised bed on the south-facing side, built of old stones from the ruins. The surrounding walls are mainly in shade and there is quite a bit of hard standing, which means planting space is limited. A terrace at the far end has some small borders and several containers to work with, but it feels important to respect the space that the building occupied and not to cover the surviving architectural features with abundant greenery.

To replicate the height and spread of the original building, a specimen magnolia *Magnolia stellata* has been planted. This becomes a cloud of white flowers in February or March, and later a shady green umbrella to punctuate the grey stone landscaping at the back. While it is still bare of leaves in winter, the white flowers of a japanese quince *Chaenomeles 'Nivalis'* clothe the wall behind. Also at the back is a viburnum *Viburnum bodnantense* and a vine which climbs around an old niche. An oak-leaved hydrangea *Hydrangea quercifolia* lolls over the terrace. It has attractive russet-coloured leaves in autumn, and its elongated creamy flower panicles make wonderful dried arrangements for indoors.

Flourishing in the raised bed (from left):
campanula and erigeron; Kaufman tulips;
aubretias and ceanothus

The south-facing raised bed unsurprisingly gets sun all day and has very sharp drainage (possibly rubble under the soil) with the result that plants either love it – or not; roses, for instance, do not. Many of the things that flourish here have blue flowers, such as Russian sage *Perovskia atriplicifolia* or Californian lilac *Ceanothus thyrsiflorus*, teasels *Diapscus fullonum*, globe thistles *Echinops ritro* and the bluey-mauve aubretias.

There are also warmer tints from the frilly orange poppy *Papaver rupifragum*, silky Californian poppies *Escholschzia californicum*, red valerian *Centranthus ruber* and the yellow drumsticks of cotton lavender *Santolina 'Lemon Queen'*, while the yarrow *Achillea 'Gold Plate'* keeps things tall and umbelliferous at the back. Towards the end of summer, a blue and orange scheme prevails. There are other plants that like it here too. In spring we grow the small yellow and pink tulip *Tulipa Kaufmanii* – as the flowers strain to catch the sun, they all lean together in a most attractive way. The sticky-leaved rockrose *Cistus landanifer* produces creamy white rounded flowers with a brown bee-guide smudge in early summer. Probably the greatest success we have ever had (some might say too great) was with the little daisy *Erigeron karvinskiana*, which we first grew from seed in 2004 and has now spread itself along the base of each wall, blending with the green mossiness of the 'mind-your-own-business' and adding a sprinkle of starry white flowers almost all year round. It can also be seen waving from the top of the 5m high walls.

BEST TIME FOR VIEWING

 All year round

Globe thistle (left) adds
height; *Hydrangea quercifolia*
on the terrace (below);
rockrose (bottom)

COLLEGE GARDEN

AT A SIZE OF JUST LESS THAN ONE acre, this is the largest of the Abbey gardens and has the reputation of being the oldest garden in England. This is where the Benedictine monks grew vegetables and had their orchards of apples and plums. They would have grown 'bitter herbs' for making the ale that was their staple drink, and vines for grapes to make wine and vinegar, as until around 1300 Britain had a more Mediterranean climate. There were also stewponds for freshwater fish; dovecotes; and beehives, which produced honey for brewing and beeswax for candles. Here too was the infirmarer's garden, growing the plants used to treat illness.

As well as providing for the bodily needs of the monks, the garden also offered spiritual comforts. It would have been beautiful to walk around, protected from the outside world as it is today. Spring flowers such as daffodils, primroses and apple blossom would have been followed by summer roses, jasmine, lilies and other flowers for the bees. A short walk through the cloister from the infirmary in St Catherine's Chapel would have allowed the aged and convalescent to sit on a bench and feel the healing rays of the sun.

The stone wall here once surrounded the garden. Built in 1374/75 to keep out trespassers and protect the crops, it would originally have been thatched with reeds, but now has a more easily-maintained capping of bricks. The west wall was replaced in 1729 by a dormitory building for Westminster School; the north wall by residents' houses. In the north-east corner, where the greenhouse now stands, a square piece of the garden appears to be missing, taken by Edward III in the fourteenth century to build his Jewel Tower.

Within the wall too there have been additions. Two clergymen's houses, now offices, were built at the southern end of the garden in the late 1800s, most probably where the stewponds once were, as

College Garden in spring, with daffodils 'February Gold' (above); the entrance border in April (right)

house

Fig

house

Gate

Ramp

MAY

Judas

White
Mulberry

↗ Compost
Heaps

Walnut

← Bunker

Planes

Meadow
Area

Mulberry

Great
White Cherry

Prunus Kanzan

Rose
Garden

Gardener's
Yard

Koelreuteria

Westminster
School

← Greenhouse

insect house

Wall

Resident's
Garden

Resident's
Garden

Herb
Garden

Iris
Garden

Vine
Garden

Entrance

we often dig up grey mud embedded with tiny fossilised crustaceans in this area. Five massive London plane trees now dominate the garden, which were planted in 1849.

A Mackenzie and Moncur 'glasshouse' was built in 1929 in the north-east corner, which is still a working greenhouse, full of seedlings and small plants in spring and summer, and pelargonium cuttings in autumn and winter. It has also offered training opportunities for horticultural students. This small area, not generally open to the public, is now the gardeners' yard, set aside for growing bedding plants and vegetables, tool maintenance and the creation of seasonal flower displays and with a pyracantha tree hanging over the yard entrance. The garden office is here, situated discreetly under a golden rain tree, *Koelreuteria*, and cut off from the rest of the garden by a wattle fence and a yew hedge. Also here is a concrete bunker, now almost entirely hidden by Boston ivy, which was built against the east wall as a bomb shelter for the residents during World War II.

Despite these changes, College Garden retains its original sense of place. It still contains the homes of people who work here and so it has a community feel. The residents walk their dogs here, the students of Westminster School take lessons and revise here, there are summer workshops for children, band concerts and charity fund-raising events. Yet sometimes – on a misty morning in February when the daffodils are out around the trees and a robin is singing – you can almost see a few monks carrying out their work, and hear the waters of the Thames and the Tyburn lapping just outside the walls.

When I arrived here, I wanted to capture the essence of a monastery garden – a wonderful anachronism right opposite the Houses of Parliament – but

Right: South Transept and quince tree
Below left to right: bluebells and tulips; daisies and dandelions in the meadow area; formal bed with irises

Right: Jan at work inside the greenhouse

ROSE GARDEN

The Rose Garden was created in 2002 to celebrate HM The Queen's Golden Jubilee, forming a floral focus to the right of the entrance. It features a central cupola topped by a golden ball, surrounded by concentric hedges of hornbeam and box.

The roses, both standard and climbing, grow beside the winding path, interspersed with lavender, clematis and bulbs, which include statuesque alliums.

The view opposite shows clematis 'Josephine' keeping the colour going on the cupola once the climbing rose has finished, with alliums encircling the whole.

at the same time to make a garden that could welcome visitors all year round. In every direction were elegant formal buildings, but I wanted to include something of the meadow that once existed here. There would be neat hedges and topiaried yew and box, but also breezy campions and campanulas, delicate aquilegias and love-in-a-mist, with bright poppies weaving their way through everything. There was already a 'meadow area', a small mound on the lawn dotted with crocus, fritillaries and bluebells, where the grass was left long until June.

When choosing the plants, I had to take the prevailing conditions into consideration. In many ways these are positive: the surrounding walls and buildings preserve a microclimate two degrees higher than that outside it; the top end of the garden basks in sun all summer long; and the fertile soil is wonderfully easy to dig. The big problem is dryness, whether in

FORMAL GARDEN

At the southern end of College Garden is a more formal area with paving and a fountain. Shaded by a white mulberry tree and in part raised slightly above the level of the main garden, it is a good place to sit and enjoy the view. Laurel hedges, combined with statues and other architectural salvage from the Abbey, add to the sense of permanence.

In spring it comes alive with tulips and other spring bulbs, while in summer we light it up with colourful planters.

sun or shade, for the buildings and trees take up nearly all the available water. We have learnt to grow plants that can cope with near-drought conditions and, by applying compost to the borders every spring, we have also been able to grow more moisture-loving plants such as ferns.

Introducing some standard quince trees and six step-over apple trees to the entrance border was one of the first things we did, going on to grow vegetables in there too, red-flowered broad beans and cabbages along with the wallflowers. Visitors love seeing edible plants growing alongside the flowers and it is also a practical way of getting bees to pollinate your vegetables. It seems to fit the garden perfectly.

BEST TIME FOR VIEWING

 Winter for scented shrubs and trees; spring for bulbs and cherry blossom; summer for the Herb Garden and roses.

Right: irises in the corner bed, looking towards the entrance to the garden

HERB GARDEN

THE HERB GARDEN IS A RECENT development inside College Garden, opened in 2010. It is divided into four main beds, for culinary herbs, medicinal herbs, dye plants and vegetables, with roses and sweet peas in the central fifth bed. Around the edges are strewing plants, forming a living potpourri. The chamomile turf seats on either side at the back of the garden are based on a medieval idea: somewhere cool to sit while fully appreciating the sweet scent. These and the wattle edging are made of woven willow. This is a very hot and sunny part of College Garden, which suits most herbs well. All kinds of bees and butterflies enjoy this garden, attracted to the simple flowers, which also helps with the pollination of flowers and vegetables.

In monastic times, these fragrant plants would have been used to make life more pleasant indoors. Strewing rosemary, woodruff or southernwood on the floor acted as an air freshener and insect repellant. In places where the odours were especially noxious, like courtrooms and prisons, the herb rue was used. Culinary herbs were used to flavour cooking, as there were few other ways of making the restricted diet palatable. Some herbs such as tansy that we would find too pungent were used to flavour cakes and puddings. The strong acid taste of sorrel was also popular. Vegetables grown included members of the onion family, such as leeks, and kale or cabbage. Diet was also used by monks to heal sickness. Medicinal herbs were chosen either for

efficacy or because they fitted in with the doctrine of signatures, the idea that the natural remedy looked like the diseased part of the body in need of treatment. Hence lungwort, *Pulmonaria*, with its spotted leaves, was thought to resemble diseased lungs and was used accordingly.

Today the garden produce is gathered by the residents for their meals, and is also used in workshops for school parties studying monastic life, cookery and insect identification. A side-benefit of herbs is that many are also 'wildflowers' and therefore attractive to ladybirds and bees.

Above: summer vegetables in the Herb Garden
Below: The culinary herb bed

A selection of the culinary, medicinal and dye plants and vegetables grown in the Herb Garden, including the chamomile turf seat (centre top)

CURRY PLANT *Helichrysum italicum*

The rather modern scent of the curry plant was loved by the Elizabethans. It was planted along path edges, so that the long dresses of the ladies brushed against it, stimulating its exotic scent. Also used as an insect repellant.
Interesting fact: this plant is related to *'immortelles'* or everlasting flowers; oil extracted from them has anti-ageing properties.

SWEET WOODRUFF
Galium odoratum

When picked and dried for a few days, sprigs of this plant give off the scent of new-mown hay – a sweet, grassy smell. It can also be used in small amounts in summer punches or puddings.
Interesting fact: the 'ruff' in the name refers to the way the leaves are arranged around the stem.

SOUTHERNWOOD *Artemisia abrotanum*

The pungent scent of this grey-leaved plant is best for repelling moths.
Interesting fact: it is related to wormwood, used to make the drink absinthe.

HYSSOP
Hyssopus officinalis

A valuable medicinal herb used by the monks as an infusion to treat coughs and bronchitis.
Also has antibacterial properties.
Interesting fact: this small evergreen plant, with blue, white or pink flowers, makes an attractive low-growing hedge around a border.

YARROW *Achillea millefolium*

The leaves were laid on wounds to help them heal, as Achilles is said to have done. Can also be used as an infusion to bring down fever.
Interesting fact: *millefolium*, meaning 'thousand leaves', describes the finely feathered leaves, too many to count.

LOVAGE *Levisticum officinale*

A delicious ingredient to use in salads or sandwiches, particularly with eggs or potatoes.
Interesting fact: it is not available to buy so you will have to grow it yourself. It grows to 2m tall and has long roots, dying down in winter and coming back in spring.

STRAWBERRY *Fragaria x annannassa*

Sunburn can be soothed by rubbing a strawberry on the affected area.
Interesting fact: the 'straw' in the name comes from their habit of 'strewing' themselves as they grow – throwing out a long stem with a small plant at the end of it.

TREES AND SHRUBS

TREES

MAY OR MIDLAND HAWTHORN *Crataegus laevigata*
This stands by the back gate, recalling the thorn
trees which gave Thorney Island its name. The
flowers, which emerge in May, are red on the
outside and white in the middle, the bark has a
golden sheen to it and the long thorns are to be
avoided when pruning. The young leaves used
to be eaten when there were few other greens
available, and the 'haws' are sources of vitamin C
and can be used in hedgerow jam.

FIRETHORN PYRACANTHA *'Orange Glow'*
There is an unusual specimen of this tree near
to the greenhouse. It has very twisted branches,
which make it look as if it has been carefully
trained, but they are natural and offer cover for

From left below:
*Pyracantha
'Orange Glow'*;
golden rain tree
with the Victoria
Tower behind;
fig tree in winter;
golden rain tree
in flower

the garden's birdbath. It has very small oval evergreen leaves and white blossom in May, followed by orange berries in September. It also has thorns. Firethorn berries can also be red or yellow, and it is from the effect of these that it gets its name.

GOLDEN RAIN TREE
Koelreuteria paniculata
This hangs over the garden office. If it is windy, the branches knock on the roof in a comforting way as I'm doing paperwork. It originally comes from China, where its large black seeds were used to make ink, and is one of the trees featured on the English willow pattern ceramics inspired by Chinese imports. It does not grow too large and has attractive notched leaves, which are salmon pink in spring, fresh green in summer and yellow in autumn. It produces long yellow 'panicles' of flowers in summer and papery seed cases shaped like lanterns in the autumn.

FIG *Ficus carica*
The large specimen at the bottom of College Garden leans forward so much it has to be supported by a metal prop. Its trunk is covered in huge warty lumps and its hand-shaped leaves are especially large. There is a convenient bench placed below it and it is the coolest place to sit on a hot summer day. Its fruit never ripens, as it is in too shady a position, but it looks good all year round, even in winter with snow on its branches – and its leaves make the best compost.

KOWHAI *Sophora microphylla*
These evergreen trees from New Zealand have small pea-like leaves and shoot up against the side of a large building near the back gate of College Garden. The butter-yellow flowers, which appear in February, gleam out from the brickwork of the wall. The seed pods are interesting too, like sections of a necklace.

HIMALAYAN BIRCH *Betula utilis 'Jacquemontii'*
There is a small group of birch trees behind the fountain with exceptionally white bark. Apart from the winter interest this provides, their small kite-shaped leaves shake in the breeze in a delightful way and change to gold in autumn, which looks wonderful against a blue sky.

SNAKEBARK MAPLE *Acer davidii*
These maples are unusual in having plain, almost cherry-like leaves, not the usual five-pointed kind. The main feature of these is the snakeskin patterning of the bark. The leaves turn the attractive autumnal red of other maples.

ORNAMENTAL SHRUBS

VIBURNUM DAVIDII

An evergreen shrub which is ideal for growing under house windows as it does not grow too tall. Here it grows beneath the windows of an architect's office at the bottom of College Garden. It has extremely handsome leaves – large, matt and pale-veined – and produces white flowers in spring, then blue berries.

OREGON GRAPE *Mahonia aquifolium*

While often described as a 'carpark plant', this is the shrub to use in inaccessible places. We have a group of these in a border next to the ramp leading to the back gate; they just need to be shortened every few years to keep them neat, and reward us with fragrant yellow flowers every April.

WINTERSWEET *Chimonanthus praecox*

This uninspiring-looking shrub brought itself to my attention as I was walking around Cambridge Botanic Garden on a beautiful day in February. The 'what is that delicious smell?' moment was unforgettable. Our wintersweet lives at the back of the rose garden, where its lack of visual interest is concealed. Every December/January its small greenish yellow flowers exude a cloud of exotic fragrance.

Left from top:
Viburnum davidii;
Oregon grape
(*Mahonia aquifolia*);
Winter's bark

WINTER'S BARK *Drimys winteri*

This tall gangling plant softens the façade of the Westminster School dormitory, contrasting with its classical formality. It has long waxy evergreen leaves and, for about three months in winter, creamy white star-shaped flowers. The bark was named for Captain Winter, who discovered that it treated the sailors' disease of scurvy, while he was sailing around the world with Sir Francis Drake in 1577–80. The leaves release a lime fragrance when crushed.

HONEY SPURGE *Euphorbia mellifera*

A handsome plant that is so at home in the garden it seeds itself around the borders. It has long leaves with a distinctive stripe down the middle. The flowers are strange alien-looking things, small, scaly and orange, but their wafting smell of honey in April is what it's all about. It is easy to grow in dry soil and just needs shortening to the ground when it gets too tall.

GOLDEN ELDER *Sambucus racemosa 'Sutherland Gold'*

Why don't people grow elders more? There are purple-leaved ones and lacy-leaved ones. They don't get too big, have edible flowers and fruits, are easy to grow and can be cut back without

Above left:
the towers
of the Abbey
veiled by the
flowers of
golden elder
Above right:
Wintersweet at
the back of the
Rose Garden

harm. The one thing they need is sun and that may be their downfall – they get shoved in the back of a border, overcrowded and in the shade, and don't do well. Ours is in the Herb Garden, an elegant plant that looks particularly glorious in spring when its leaves are just about to come out.

RED-LEAVED HAZEL *Corylus*

This nut-producing plant also has attractive dark red leaves and catkins. It can be used as a hedge or grown tall and then coppiced, to produce long stems valuable as plant supports. Hazel is one of our native plants, grown for centuries along with willow to produce twigs for weaving and wood for fuel; its advantage here is that it does not need the moist soil that willow requires.

CORNELIAN CHERRY *Cornus mas*

Another English native, much loved for its yellow flowers in winter. It has a distinctive growth, with new branches developing almost at right angles on either side of the stem. This is very clear in the winter, as the flowers emerge before the leaves. The sour cherries it produces in summer are edible.

JAN'S FAVOURITE FLOWERS

WINTER

WINTER ACONITE *Eranthis hyemalis*

These 10cm high yellow flowers, related to the buttercup, emerge in the depths of winter among the snowdrops. Natives of Turkey, they either like your garden or they don't; fortunately they seem to like ours. Close examination of the flowers reveals that each has a green 'collar' – smartly dressed for spring!

ELEPHANT'S EARS *Bergenia cordifolia*

At first sight, this low-growing pink-flowered, evergreen plant may look rather coarse and cabbagey; we use it as a kind of policeman at the front of our borders, to keep dead leaves and other rubbish out of them. Its flowers first appear in February, which cheers everyone up, and then again in July. If its leaves start looking tatty, they can be removed with secateurs, which is one of the nicest jobs in the garden, making a satisfying crunch as if you are chopping rhubarb.

HELLEBORE *Helleborus orientalis* 'Ashwood hybrids'

Between January and March, you will see many hellebore flowers in shades of green, purple, yellow and white. These 'flowers' are not really flowers but sepals (a kind of leaf), which last a lot longer; the actual flower is the central boss, which resembles embroidery. We have a winter display of white hellebores in the Little Cloister.

SPRING

SMYRNIUM PERFOLIATUM

These are fantastic foliage plants. Statuesque at around 1m tall, their lime green stems and leaves go beautifully with spring flowers such as bluebells, forget-me-nots and the white flowers

Clockwise from above: hellebore and sweet woodruff; *Smyrnium perfoliatum*, with *Narcissus poeticus*; *Bergenia* in the south border

of wild garlic. The whole plant is 'see-through' in the sense that it doesn't obscure anything else. The young leaves can be harvested to make a delicious cordial.

BLUE FLAG IRIS *Iris germanica*
There are many spectacular iris flowers, in all colours and levels of frilliness. *Iris germanica* has plain blue sweet-smelling flowers and is not so tall that it needs support. The foliage is sword-shaped, in a pleasing shade of blue green, which adds architecture to the border. Iris plants are the gardener's pets as they can be tended all year round.

MEADOW RUE *Thalictrum delaveyi*
This perennial was grown from seed about 10 years ago, and is still going strong. Liking a little shade, and supposedly moist conditions, it nevertheless grows happily in our dry soil. Around 60cm tall, it has attractive green-blue leaves and fluffy lilac flowers in May or June, which go perfectly with the yellow Welsh poppies and 'Johnson's blue' geraniums.

SEA KALE *Crambe maritima*
Elegant matt blue fronds like Matisse cut-outs emerge from curly buds in April, followed by honey-scented creamy white flowers in early summer. Hugely attractive to butterflies and bees and perfect to grow among your vegetables. It was popular as a vegetable in Victorian times.

WALLFLOWER 'GIANT PINK' *Erysimum cheiri*
These familiar and reliable plants are said to have come to England with William the Conqueror on blocks of Caen stone, hence the association with walls. 'Giant Pink' is an old variety with an antique pink colour that fits well here and also seems to come true from seed.

Clockwise from left: wallflower 'Giant Pink'; *Violas*, or heartsease; white bleeding heart

HEARTSEASE *Viola tricolori*
Violas, and their larger-flowered cousins, pansies, have always been popular because of their thoughtful expression – the word 'pansy' comes from the French *'pensée'*. Some have cat-like 'whiskers' marked on their petals. We also have the true native *Viola rupestris rosea* growing in the lawn of St Catherine's Chapel Garden.

BLEEDING HEART *Dicentra / Lamprocapnos spectabilis 'Alba'*
Elegant lanterns with frond-like foliage that go with everything and shine out from shade among the ferns and lily-of-the-valley. The red version is also beautiful but is more difficult to place in the garden.

41

SUMMER

ASPHODEL CRANESBILL *Geranium asphodeloides*

It's hard to exaggerate my enthusiasm for this well-behaved little front-of-border plant. Delicate, lacy, apple-green leaves obediently soften the area where border meets paving. Small medium-pink flowers appear just above them and gracefully fade to white – this graduated colour palette gives them added interest. To keep the mat looking neat, it can be cut back almost to ground level with shears in July. Likes semi-shade.

THRIFT *Armeria maritima*

It is perhaps not surprising that this native of clifftops should be happy growing in a sunny, dry garden. It grows in hummocks, its pointed leaves making them look like small green hedgehogs. Diminutive pink drumstick flowers wave above them in early summer, and can be deadheaded for continuous flowers. There is a white-flowered version but it is not as vigorous.

ROSE *Rosa 'Madame Sancy de Parabère'*

This is a cultivated rose which I went in person to choose from David Austin Roses, as it was to be the centrepiece of the Rose Garden. It was recommended to me in a broad Black Country accent, which is how I always pronounce it in my head! It is thornless, which is important as it is trained over a pergola and needs to be pruned regularly, and its flowers are neither too big nor too small and exactly the right shade of pink.

Clockwise from near left: hollyhock flower, with visiting bee; love-in-a-mist and poppies; clove pink; rose 'Madame Sancy de Parabère'; asphodel cranesbill

HOLLYHOCK *Alcea rosea*

Hollyhocks, and their smaller relations in the mallow family such as musk mallow *Malva moschata* and *Lavatera tremestris*, fit in well, with their trumpet-shaped pastel-coloured flowers. Along a sunny wall is the perfect place for the tall hollyhock. There's something about the combination of its size and cottage garden prettiness that makes it the perfect foil for church buildings.

ITALIAN SWEET PEAS *Lathyrus cupani*

Discovered by Brother Francis Cupani in Sicily in the seventeenth century, the pink and purple flowers of this plant are modest in size but highly perfumed. It is generally disease-free and fits in visually with other plants. If you can grow sweet peas 'along' rather than 'up' it causes the plants less stress, while generous watering and assiduous harvesting will prolong flowering.

LOVE-IN-A-MIST *Nigella damascena*

These generally blue, though sometimes white or pink, annuals create a misty drift of colour in sunny parts of the garden. The plants have ferny leaves, like fennel, and stay at the useful height of around 45cm. The flowers are papery with pointed petals, and the seedheads are like little minarets. The black seeds are used in cookery; when eaten fresh they smell and taste of strawberries. The plants helpfully seed themselves every year.

AUTUMN

ROSE *Rosa mutabilis*

Cultivated roses generally need a richer soil than we can give them, so we tend to grow species roses such as *Rosa rugosa*, *Rosa banksii* and *Rosa mutabilis*. The latter has flowers that change colour from peach to apricot and then to scarlet over a long season and is still flowering in December. The leaves are small and graceful with red tints. It is also relatively thornless and has decorative hips.

KAFFIR LILY *Schizostylis coccinea*

A useful bulb which produces its starry pink or red flowers from August to October. It likes hot dry conditions, and usefully spreads itself around, increasing year after year. We started off with three plants and now have over 30.

CLOVE PINK *Dianthus caryophyllus*

Unlike the florist's carnation, the home-grown flower possesses one of the most delicious scents in the garden. Pinks are one of those plants for which there was a craze in the 1700s, like tulips in the 1600s. At one time the 'gillyflower' could be given in lieu of rent. The term for the colour pink is said to come from the 'pinked' edges of the petals. Flowers all summer long, but needs a spot in the sun.

WILDLIFE

WORKING IN A LARGE GARDEN for 15 years, I have seen changes in the wildlife population. In 2000, the feral London pigeon was the most common bird but they are a rarity here these days, replaced by the wood pigeon. Their arrival coincided with our first attempts to fill the garden with vegetables – they must have been delighted to find a supply of cabbage in their new urban home.

More unusual birds have included the pair of sparrowhawks who set up home in one of the central plane trees in College Garden. Every morning, as we arrived, there would be the blood-curdling (to other birds) screech of hungry young sparrowhawks wanting breakfast. These beautiful brown-striped birds brought up two sets of young and then departed, leaving the garden with scarcely a blackbird, wren or sparrow.

Luckily for the smaller birds, they never returned. Peregrine falcons living on Victoria Tower in the Houses of Parliament concentrate their attention on pigeons, and we often find the gruesome remains – just a pair of wings lying on the lawn. Blackbirds, wrens, blue tits, great tits, robins, wood pigeons and magpies all nest in the garden. Regular visitors have included goldcrests, grey wagtails, goldfinches, long-tailed tits, woodpeckers and jays.

A pair of grey squirrels once made a nest in a hole in the medieval wall, filling it with the large leaves of a nearby *Magnolia grandiflora*. I watched them one evening, grabbing the leaves with both

tiny 'hands' and shoving them into the wall cavity. It must have made an uncomfortable nest, as they are hard inflexible leaves, and no young squirrels have ever appeared.

We also have bats. On summer evenings they can be seen circling College Garden in their quest for gnats. They have been known to appear at lunchtime on a warm day, while staff are eating their sandwiches, apparently something that happens as they come out of hibernation. They wake up because it is warm, suddenly feel hungry and, disoriented, set off in broad daylight. The tall trees and buildings provide good homes for bats.

Peacock butterfly on a strawberry leaf (below); scavenging squirrel (bottom)

Egyptian geese in the bluebells (top); wood pigeon (above)

Some years ago Dr Richard Mortimer, the Abbey's Keeper of the Muniments, alerted me to the existence of a special spider that lives in the Abbey's walls. Its Latin name is *Segestria florentina*, more appealing than its common name of 'green-jawed spider'. One of the largest spiders found in the UK, it originates in Spain or Italy and was introduced in imported crates of fruit. Our specimen, known as the 'Abbey Spider', is very shy and luckily rarely seen.

Ducks from St James's Park sometimes make nests in the compost heaps, and we then have to conduct processions of yellow or brown ducklings back to their true home by the lake there. More recently we have been visited by a charming couple of Egyptian geese we call Anthony and Cleopatra. They are extremely tame and accost the visitors, asking to share their lunch.

As I compose my diary at the end of the day, after everyone has gone home, I look out of the window. Exactly in my line of view, under the *Pyracantha* tree, is a birdbath. As often as not, around 4.00– 5.00pm is bath time. Maybe a female blackbird will start things off, splashing around, then hopping off into the tree to dry. Already a queue has formed to take her place – blue tits, wrens and robins – all waiting for a turn.

SEASONAL TASKS

Student sowing seeds in the greenhouse

Weaving a willow obelisk

A completed obelisk

Restoring cold frames

Strimming in College Garden

Trimming the vine in College Garden

Laying turf in Little Cloister Garden

Mowing in St Catherine's Chapel Garden

Jan trimming the dogwood in College Garden

Pruning the quince trees in College Garden

PLANS FOR THE FUTURE

AS PART OF A PROGRAMME OF REPAIRS RESULTING FROM THE QUINQUEN-NIAL report, many of the Abbey's green areas have recently been out of bounds, covered by building compounds or scaffolding. Part of the gardener's role is to see these changes as an opportunity to make improvements to the Abbey's green areas as they are repaired. The area around Poets' Corner, for example, has been a scrubby stretch of grass in the past, but now will be properly landscaped around the lift to the new Queen's Diamond Jubilee Galleries in the triforium.

Some exciting developments have been happening in College Garden, with the repointing of the medieval wall and the painstaking replacement of the capping all the way round. This will eventually arrive at the greenhouse, which will have to be temporarily dismantled. The greenhouse roof can then be repaired, as it has leaked for some time, and the whole structure improved, to help us grow a wider variety of plants. We would then be better placed to offer work-placements to horticultural students – at the moment only three people can sit in our bothy at once!

A garden is an ongoing piece of design brought about by both choice and necessity. Nothing is fixed, unlike buildings, but we hope the gardens of Westminster Abbey will always provide a unique and enjoyable experience to those who visit them.